So, You Want to Be The Boss Now?
15 Steps to Start, Run, and Grow Your Own Business

Do you have what it takes to run your own business? Do you have the right mindset? Can you envision your success and the impact your company will have in the world? Can you build a team that holds you accountable, tells the truth, and keeps you grounded? Are you equipped to be the Boss?

In this Itty Bitty® book, Gregory Allan Datu Cendana provides you with the tools to:

- Establish Your Mission, Vision, Theory of Change, and Values
- Create a Solid Financial Plan
- Build a Team and Map Your Network
- Develop Your Brand
- Incorporate Diversity, Inclusion, Equity, and Justice
- Be The Boss Now!

Pick up a copy of this exciting Itty Bitty® book and start your own adventure of becoming the Boss of your own company today.

Your Amazing Itty Bitty® Be the Boss Now Book

15 Key Steps to Start, Run, and Grow Your Own Business

Gregory Allan Datu Cendana

Published by Itty Bitty® Publishing
A Subsidiary of S & P Productions, Inc.

Copyright © 2021 **Gregory Allan Datu Cendana**

All rights reserved. No part of this book may be reproduced or transmitted in any form or by any means, electronic or mechanical, including photocopying, recording or by any information storage and retrieval system, without written permission of the publisher, except for inclusion of brief quotations in a review.

Printed in the United States of America.

Itty Bitty Publishing
311 Main Street, Suite D
El Segundo, CA 90245
(310) 640-8885

ISBN: 978-1-950326-86-0

Dedication Page

For my family, friends, educators, and anyone—including the naysayers—who played a role in shaping the boss that I am today.

For you and everyone with an idea of starting a business who may not know where to start or were told that you are not worthy, let this book be your guide, light, and motivation. We all can be the boss NOW.

Stop by our Itty Bitty® website to find more interesting information regarding ...

www.IttyBittyPublishing.com

Or visit Gregory Allan Datu Cendana at:

www.BeTheBossNow.com or
www.CSWSconsulting.com

Table of Contents

Introduction
- Step 1. Believe in Yourself and Shift Your Mindset—You Can Do This!
- Step 2. Envision Your Success and What Change Your Company Will Make in the World
- Step 3. Be Clear on Your Audience and What You'll Tell Them About Why You Are Equipped to Be the Boss
- Step 4. Establish Your Mission, Vision, Theory of Change, and Values to Tell the Story of Your Company
- Step 5. Making it Official: One Time You'll Be Happy to Hear from the IRS
- Step 6. Figure Out the Finances Because the Money You Earn Has to Go Somewhere
- Step 7. Build a Team That Holds You Accountable, Tells the Truth, and Keeps You Grounded
- Step 8. Develop a Brand That Matches Your Energy and Gets People Pumped
- Step 9. Map Your Networks and Explore Thought Leaders in Your Field
- Step 10. Incorporate Diversity, Inclusion, Equity, and Justice
- Step 11. Announce Publicly to the World That You Are a Boss
- Step 12. Get Paid Your Worth and Negotiate: You Will Never Know Unless You Ask

Step 13.	Rest and Rejuvenation Are Needed to Be a Boss
Step 14.	Build a Leadership Pipeline and Open the Door for Others
Step 15.	Stay Humble and Remember There Is Always Something to Learn

Introduction

Starting at a young age, I had an entrepreneurial spirit. I sold cups of Kool-Aid or lemonade on the sidewalk with my neighbors. When Discmans and boom boxes were still a thing, I made compilation albums with the biggest hits of that time. As part of my dance team and student government in high school, we sold candy bars or overpriced catalog merchandise to fundraise for class trips, uniforms, and travel costs for competitions or showcases.

Of course, this spirit was fed by the sacrifice and resilience of my immigrant parents, Maria and John Cendana, who made sure my sister, Jessica, and I could have a better life and the opportunities to live our dreams.

One of those dreams for me was starting my own company. In 2009, along with Carmen Berkley, we co-founded Can't Stop! Won't Stop! Consulting with no previous business experience or inheritance. We believed it was important to see more people who looked like us and shared our values in leadership positions, influencing policy and thriving in a world where there were limitless possibilities. Little did we know what this dream for a better future would mean for a budding firm and the ongoing roles we would play.

After serving as a non-profit executive for more than 10 years at two different national organizations, I decided to take the consulting firm full-time, and Carmen became the first official board member. Feeling both excited for the opportunity and terrified about the unknown, there were, and continue to be many lessons, struggles, and reasons to celebrate along the way.

After going through the process, finding my stride, and being able to look back, this is the book I wish I had when it all began. I hope it is a useful resource for you.

Step 1
Believe in Yourself and Shift Your Mindset—You Can Do This!

Too many people have ideas for companies and more times than not, they are usually in their own way. I am here to tell you that it is not only possible, but you CAN make your dream come true and be the boss NOW. Through it all, the most important shift is within yourself. Your mind is one of the greatest tools you have, and this book will help you focus it to build your own successful business.

1. Decide that you are ready to be a boss. Affirm to yourself that you can and will become a boss.
2. Read daily affirmations.
3. Verbalize affirmations and speak them into existence.
4. Repeat. As the saying goes, if you do not believe in yourself, how will somebody else believe in you?
5. As you sharpen the practice of daily affirmations, write your own based on personal experiences and what will motivate you to your fullest potential.

Examples of Affirmations:

- I am ready to be the boss now.
- I am loved, loving, and lovable.
- I am thankful for what I have and what is yet to come.
- I am powerful. I am power.
- I can live my best life without tearing others down.
- I deserve joy and happiness. We all deserve joy and happiness.
- I trust myself and my instincts above anyone else.
- I will dance like no one is watching.
- I am ready to be the boss now. (Yes, it's true!)

While these particular affirmations are written using "I" statements, it may help to turn them into "you" statements, especially if you are looking in the mirror or recording them on your phone or another device.

Step 2
Envision Your Success and What Change Your Company Will Make in the World

Once you change your mindset, you will unlock the ability to imagine new possibilities and begin the journey of starting your own company. The next step is to envision your success and how your company will change you, your community, and the world.

1. Start with yourself and use the concept of the five human senses: sight, hearing, smell, taste, and touch.
2. Close your eyes and take deep breaths through your nose and breathe out through your mouth to help you feel grounded.
3. Remember, this is how *you* define success or winning for yourself, not what a family member or friend says, or what you see on the news or social media.
4. Now imagine your company is up and running and ask yourself, how does it change you? How will your community or the world be different as people experience your company? How does success look, sound, smell, taste, or feel like for your company and when you are the boss?

Capturing Your Visions:

These visioning exercises should bring up multiple feelings, ideas, and concepts. Find a way to capture them all. Here are some ideas:

- Write in a journal or start a blog.
- Develop a vision board.
- Make a video or vlog.
- Create a dance, painting, sketch, or some other form of art.
- Share your ideas with loved ones and put a short skit together.

If there is anything life has taught me, including through a global pandemic, it's that there is more we can do to improve the lives of everyone, especially for those who are the most vulnerable and marginalized. This step provides you with a destination for your roadmap and can keep you grounded as you go through the rest of the process.

Step 3
Be Clear on Your Audience and What You'll Tell Them About Why You Are Equipped to Be the Boss

Now that you have shifted your mindset and unlocked your wildest dreams and aspirations, it is time to start getting into the tactical pieces of your company. To start, figure out who your target audience is. Who will be using the services or goods that you will provide?

1. It is important that you identify and specify demographic areas, geographies, or experiences that you want to target. For example, are you hoping to reach out to folks of a particular race, ethnicity, age, city or region? What about parents, artists, non-profit leaders, or those in specific sectors?
2. As you determine each of your audiences, write audience-specific messages that will feature services or goods your company will provide.

Guidance for Your Messages and Offerings:

- Speak to your audience's interests, especially if there are specific ways you can serve their needs.
- Your life experiences make you an expert in certain areas. Weave those into your business purpose and mission, as long as you provide the context and credit that establish soundness and validity.
- Share what clients get from you or your company that is different than other companies.
- Be honest about your capacity—what you can or cannot do. People appreciate someone who is upfront and will not agree just for the sake of a sale.
- Accept the reality that not everyone will be your customer or partner and that is okay.

Your goal should be focused on quality versus quantity—what you can do to ensure your client's experience will be positive, memorable, and worthwhile.

Step 4
Establish Your Mission, Vision, Theory of Change, and Values to Tell the Story of Your Company

After determining your audience, the next step is to establish your company's mission, vision, theory of change, and values. These elements are important to keep your company focused and they will help you make decisions as you start, run, and grow your company.

1. Your mission is the definition of what your company does and why your company exists. This should also include the definition of your audience.
2. Your vision is the description of the future you want to create and should be aspirational in nature.
3. Your theory of change is the strategies and approaches you will take and why your company will be effective in implementing them.
4. Your values are the principles that will guide how you will operationalize the above in your company.

Tips as You Write Your Mission, Vision, Theory of Change, and Values

- These statements should be succinct, inspirational, and easy to comprehend. Try sharing with a colleague, family member or friend as a temperature check and to get guidance on potential changes. In the best-case scenario, test it out on someone who is in your target audience.
- It is likely you will use these on your website, in talks you give at conferences, during pitch meetings, or in quick elevator rides. Be clear about what each element means to you personally; they become collateral that clients will count on.
- These talking points can shift as you go along but having a starting place and landing points to refer to are key.

Step 5
Making it Official: One Time You'll Be Happy to Hear from the IRS

You are now in a good place to make your company official by applying for an employee identification number (EIN) from the Internal Revenue Service (IRS) and registering with your local or state government agency.

1. An EIN or FEIN (Federal Employer Identification Number) is used to identify your company. There is no cost to apply, and you can do it online.
2. You will also need to register with your Secretary of State, business bureau, or relevant economic development agency. As a District of Columbia business owner, I worked with the Department of Consumer and Regulatory Affairs (DCRA). Be sure to find out what is required in your state or jurisdiction.
3. You will need to determine what corporate and legal structure to use. There are several different options; I chose an LLC or Limited Liability Company.

Business Structures to Consider

- C (General) for-profit corporation
- S (Small) for-profit corporation
- Nonprofit corporation
- Limited partnership
- Limited liability company (LLC)
- Limited liability partnership (LLP)
- Cooperative association
- Business statutory trust
- Sole proprietorship
- General proprietorship

Note: Depending on your structure and the services you intend to provide, you may need additional licenses and permits.

I still remember waiting hours in line at the DCRA, saving up for the fee, and paying an extra charge for them to expedite the process. This is something that can be done by an attorney to save you time. While it was one of the harder steps to navigate, it was also one of the more gratifying ones. There is something about seeing the name of your company on official paperwork from the IRS and a local or state agency. This is one time where you will be happy to get something from the IRS.

Step 6
Figure Out the Finances Because the Money You Earn Has to Go Somewhere

Now it's about time to figure out the finances and open a business bank account. This makes it possible to accept or make payments and to comply with necessary regulations.

1. At a minimum, have your Employer Identification Number (EIN) and your incorporation documents on hand. Depending on the financial institution, you may need additional information.
2. Make a list of business expenses you think you will incur. From staff or consultants to supplies and advertising to travel and banking, legal or other fees, this will be the foundation of your budget. A budget shows you how much you need to earn and what you may need to charge for your services or products.
3. I also recommend applying for a business credit card. This will help you keep track of business expenses and earn points or cash rewards on all your purchases.

Remember, You Are Not Alone

- Do not worry if this is your first time opening an account, creating a budget, or applying for a business credit card. Not everyone has the same knowledge or starting point, and there are tons of resources by searching online.
- Building these systems and processes now will make things easier for future planning and growth. Take things one step at a time.
- This is the early phase that has discouraged many in the past, though having this book already puts you in a better position.

Step 7
Build a Team That Holds You Accountable, Tells the Truth, and Keeps You Grounded

While there are ways to manage this process alone, my recommendation is that you do not. Build a team that calls you in when you are falling off track and tells you the truth even if it is not what you want to hear. The team keeps you grounded and helps you see the big picture and the success, and potential challenges, of your company.

1. As you are growing, assemble a board, cabinet, or circle of advisors. These are people who can provide guidance on your overall strategy, business plan, or potential stakeholders.
2. When you begin to have resources, consider hiring full- or part-time staff, consultants, or independent contractors.
3. There may also be volunteers willing to provide feedback on a product or idea that could help form decisions about your company. Be mindful to provide incentives or compensation for their time and labor.

Who to Consider for Your Team

- Look for people who are skilled or have experience in areas you need. Examples include strategic planning and organizational development, budget and finance, talent and human resources, program implementation, people and project management, communications, and public relations.
- Influencers or those with a track record in your sector or field.
- Those you trust and have a strong relationship with, including positive communication and open feedback.
- Representation from your target audience or people directly impacted by the problem you are trying to solve.

From my experience, making the ask encouraged me to be clear on what I wanted the "askee's" role to be and how I hoped they would contribute both as a member of my team and as an individual.

Step 8
Develop a Brand That Matches Your Energy and Gets People Pumped

At this point, there should be enough infrastructure for your business to start thinking about its brand and how it appears to the rest of the world. It should match the boldness of the company's purpose, your audacious leadership, and the energy you want to give off to get people pumped about you being the boss. Here are some critical elements.

1. Design a logo.
2. Determine engagement, which can include email, social media, in-person and/or virtual meetups.
3. Develop a website, business cards, slide deck, and other promotional materials.

Questions to Answer for Your Pitch:

It is also important you establish your pitch, which will be used with any of the items listed on the previous page (15). Your pitch should answer the following:
- Who are you?
- What problem are you solving? This will be an opportunity to impress your audience with how deeply you have thought about a problem they may be facing.
- What's the solution you or your company will provide?
- Who is the target audience?
- How did you adapt to COVID-19 or anything else that may have impacted your business?
- Why are you ready to be the boss now? Share with your audience the qualifications you have to run the business you are in and why you are well positioned to be the boss.

Depending on who you are giving the pitch to and how much time you are given—taking a short elevator ride with someone or presenting at a meeting with a potential investor—there will be different ways to shorten and sharpen the story you will share. Remember that the visuals are just as critical to get people excited about what you are bringing. Be sure to make it all pop.

Step 9
Map Your Networks and Explore Thought Leaders in Your Field

One of your biggest assets as a boss is your network. An important step in building and growing your company is mapping the people you know, look up to, and want to learn from. Make a list and put them in at least one of the following categories:

1. Family and friends: People you know from growing up, life experiences, or those already in your immediate circle of support.
2. Ideal audience: People in your sector or market; those you hope will buy your products or services.
3. Peers: Those in your sector or market who have a shared experience.
4. Thought leaders: Those who have been in the game, have a track record of success, or are directly impacted.
5. Outside the box inspiration: People not in your line of work who you can go to for motivation, grounding, or a reset.

Activate Your Networks

Now that you have a list of folks to engage, make sure you compile the necessary contact information to communicate with them, and understand what your ask will be. This is critical as it should be specific to the person, what you are looking for as it relates to your company, and how you will determine the rollout (which we will talk about in step 11). The types of asks you can make:

- Feedback on your product, service, or brand.
- Donation of time, talent, or treasure: will they give you money, in-kind designing, legal advice or an item critical for your company—maybe a lawnmower, laptop, or software—you won't have to buy?
- Participate in a focus group or trial run.
- Share your business offerings with their networks that may be interested.
- Sign up for your email list or follow you or your company on social media.

For this exercise, I went through my phone book, friend list on social media platforms, and did research for my sector and market to cast a wide net. Prepare for some people who will say no, not be interested, or those who will also inspire even greater ideas. The bigger the list the more potential you have in getting people to see your vision, why you are a boss, and how they could support you.

Step 10
Incorporate Diversity, Inclusion, Equity, and Justice

No matter what your company does, it will help to incorporate diversity, inclusion, equity, and justice on the front end.

1. Diversity: How do you ensure representation from different backgrounds, experiences, and identities? Does your team and those in your company reflect the diversity of the audience you are trying to reach?
2. Inclusion: How are typically excluded people or communities brought into your company's programs, systems, and processes like program/product development, policymaking, and budget allocation?
3. Equity: How will you ensure equal access and work to eradicate bias and discrimination? How is equity built into the process, outcomes, and people in your company?
4. Justice: How is fairness, protecting, respecting, and expanding civil and human rights part of your company?

Ways to Incorporate Diversity, Inclusion, Equity, and Justice

- From the board to staff, consultants, and the clients you work with, prioritize leaders who are Black, Indigenous, Asian, Pacific Islander, Latina/e/x/o or organizations who engage, are led, and grounded by these communities.
- Growing a company during a pandemic taught me important lessons to around access. Examples include providing closed captioning, American Sign Language or other language interpretation, and image descriptions as well as having accessibility coordinators. These are some of the ways we are practicing what we preach.
- Provide pro bono or discount services or products to directly impacted communities and non-profit organizations that are on the cutting edge of diversity, inclusion, equity, and justice.

In light of the uprisings in defense of Black life, ongoing violence in communities, and efforts of organizers, advocates, and activists around the country, there have been increased efforts to advance diversity, inclusion, equity, and justice. If your company does not include it now, it is likely to come up in the future. Do yourself a favor and act now. You will be a better and more successful boss because of it.

Step 11
Announce Publicly to the World That You Are a Boss

It may seem like there are many steps before getting to this point but to start, build, and grow your company has to be an intentional and well-thought-out process. The more time you spend preparing, the more time you will save in the future. Can you feel it? You are now at the stage to announce publicly to the world that you are a boss. Here are some facets of a launch that you may want to consider:

1. Host an event (in person or virtually).
2. Set up a website or blog.
3. Offer an incentive.
4. Engage an influencer.
5. Partner with an organization that works with your target audience.
6. Provide a testimonial from someone who can talk about your product, service, or you as a boss.
7. Send out a media advisory and press release.

Other Considerations for Your Announcement

- Remember to use this as an opportunity to share your story about why you are ready to be a boss and what led you to start this company in the first place.
- This will be the first way you will create a splash for your business, and it should be a special one.
- This does not have to be your only intervention, and through this launch you may garner interest from folks who you did not even think about or imagine in the first place.
- You don't have to do this on your own. Remember the team of people you have built and ask them to take on roles.

Now that you have let people in on your bold ideas to change the world and they know you are a boss now, this is not the time to let up. Maintain focus on your goals, what success means to you, and leverage the momentum for your company. Remember, you are a boss.

Step 12
Get Paid Your Worth and Negotiate: You Will Never Know Unless You Ask

As you get clients and begin to build relationships with people over time, you will begin to understand your worth and refine how much you are charging for your product or service. Here are some things to consider as you figure out what to ask for:

1. Be mindful of the budget for the person or organization you are working with. Obviously, there is a difference between an individual contractor who is just starting their company versus a well-established brand that has been around for decades with a larger budget.
2. It does not hurt to make the ask—you will never know if you could get paid the rate you feel you deserve if you don't ask.
3. Once you get paid a higher rate, you should ask for that moving forward. This is not to say folks will not push back, but people should know what you have been paid as part of the negotiation.

More Money Does Not Necessarily Mean Fewer Problems

To be honest, this was a challenging part of my entrepreneurial experience. As someone who grew up in a working-class family and had minimum wage jobs for multiple years in my life, I had a complicated relationship with money. Some things I learned along the way:

- There are many ways to give back to people or organizations that you care about and want to support.
- It is okay if you want to donate or offer reduced rates to pay it forward but do not let this be your only approach, as it may interrupt your business development, longer-term goals, and growth.
- Refer to your budget and your financial goals for the year—will you be able to meet those goals?
- Consider going out of your comfort zone and experiment in places or with clients you haven't worked with before.

Do not be hard on yourself as you navigate the multiple feelings that may come with money, negotiation, and getting paid. You are a boss and will be able to find the right balance as you get more experience.

Step 13
Rest and Rejuvenation Are Needed to Be a Boss

To start, grow, and build your own company, it is going to take a lot of energy, work, and time. I put in a lot of hours and admittedly, made many sacrifices. One of the biggest lessons I learned was that rest and rejuvenation are needed to be a boss. Here are some offerings on how you can do this:

1. Turn on your favorite jam and dance (my personal favorite).
2. Schedule meals, breaks, and rest time, including naps. Add them to your calendar.
3. Do breathing exercises or meditate.
4. Take a walk or go for a hike or run.
5. Paint, color, or do something else utilizing art and creativity.
6. Avoid waking up or going to sleep on your phone or an electronic device.
7. Read a book or listen to a podcast.
8. Prepare a meal or eat your favorite snack.
9. Write a song, poem, or an entry in a journal.
10. Play a video or board game.

Dimensions of Health and Wellness

Another way to think about this is to ensure your health and wellness in each of the following areas:

- Emotional
- Environmental
- Financial
- Mental or intellectual
- Physical
- Political
- Social
- Spiritual

When you are self-aware, taking care of yourself and your loved ones, and being as holistic as possible, the better boss you will be able to be, the bigger your company can grow, and the more you—and all of your people—can win.

Step 14
Build a Leadership Pipeline and Open the Door for Others

One of the most important steps to being a boss is building a leadership pipeline and opening the door for others. As you move into your leadership, ask yourself the following questions:

1. How are you making sure that someone else can have the opportunity to start, run, and grow their own company?
2. What can you do to ensure more people can also be the boss now?
3. Who do you know that has potential and with some support can also be on this journey of entrepreneurship?
4. What are the biggest lessons you learned from the process that you want to share with others?
5. How will you leverage your platform and networks to support new people trying to also be a boss?
6. When you are given an opportunity, how will you ensure someone else is also able to benefit?

The Best Boss Builds Other Bosses

The reality is that we all can be the boss and you now have the steps to make it happen. Not only can you be the boss, but others can also be bosses and we all can be more powerful together.

- There is no shortage of resources—you can start, build, and grow your company and many other people can and should be able to as well.
- There are ways to partner and support each other's companies.
- At the very least, there could be lessons learned and best practices imparted when you share your leadership success stories.

The best bosses help others understand and reach their full potential. You can be an even stronger boss if you are surrounded by other bosses.

Step 15
Stay Humble and Remember There Is Always Something to Learn

The final step of being a boss is simple. Stay humble and remember there is always something to learn from everyone you meet. As a person who valued education and had the opportunity to graduate from the University of California, Los Angeles, and serve as the President of the United States Student Association, I am committed to being a lifelong student. Here are some reasons you would want to do this as well:

1. When you are being too cocky, you allow yourself to block gifts from others you meet along your journey. You may inadvertently miss a blessing or game-changing lesson.
2. See it as a way to hone your skills and deepen your analysis—people can either push you to believe more strongly in what you feel or open your mind to other perspectives.
3. People will remember you making them feel welcome, that you care about what they have to offer, and will pass on that positive energy to the next person they meet. It will have a ripple effect.

Continue Your Learning Journey

You may be asking though, *what might this look like?* Here are some examples:

- Read the reviews or feedback that people leave, particularly if it is constructive, and receive it with an open heart and mind.
- Engage anyone you meet with kindness and respect, including those who are not directly related to your business. This could be a restaurant worker, rideshare driver, a stranger you bump into while you are out, or a customer service representative.
- Ask questions and push those around you to think critically about your product or services.
- Read more books or articles, take classes, or participate in training.
- Surround yourself with other bosses.

Being the boss can oftentimes be an isolating experience. It can be true that you can start, run, and grow your own business and do so with a community that has the ability to thrive. You can be proud of yourself for taking these steps, and I look forward to how we can push each other into further greatness. How does it feel for you to be the boss NOW?

You've finished. Before you go ...

Tweet/share that you finished this book. Use the hashtag: #BeTheBossNow and follow @GregoryCendana and @CSWSconsulting across all social media platforms.

Please star rate this book.

Reviews are solid gold to writers. Please take a few minutes to give us some itty bitty feedback.

ABOUT THE AUTHOR

Dancer, strategist, and entrepreneur Gregory Allan Datu Cendana is president and co-founder of Can't Stop! Won't Stop! Consulting, Chief Creative Officer of Greg Dances and co-founder of The People's Collective for Justice and Liberation.

He was the first openly gay and youngest-ever Executive Director of the Asian Pacific American Labor Alliance and founding Executive Director of the Institute for Asian Pacific American Leadership and Advancement. Gregory was also the first openly gay and first Filipino American Chair of the National Council of Asian Pacific Americans, co-founder of the diversity initiative Inclusv and former president of the United States Student Association (USSA), where he played an integral role in the passage of the Student Aid and Fiscal Responsibility Act and Healthcare and Education Reconciliation Act.

He has been named one of Washington DC's most influential 40-and-under young leaders, one of the 30 Most Influential Asian Americans Under 30, 40 Influential Asian Americans in Washington, DC's Inaugural Power 30 Under 30™ Award Recipients, a Capital Pride Hero and the "Future of DC Politics." In his spare time, Gregory enjoys singing karaoke, choreographing dances and trying new recipes. Follow him on Twitter and Instagram: @GregoryCendana and TikTok: @GregDances.

If you enjoyed this Itty Bitty® book you might also like…

- **Your Amazing Itty Bitty® Business Experts Compilation Book** – Various Authors

- **Your Amazing Itty Bitty® Health and Wellness Experts Compilation Book** – Various Authors

- **Your Amazing Itty Bitty® Holistic Experts Compilation Book** – Various Authors

Or the many other Itty Bitty® books available on line at www.ittybittypublishing.com.

www.ingramcontent.com/pod-product-compliance
Lightning Source LLC
Chambersburg PA
CBHW052127110526
44592CB00013B/1787